EXPLORING
WORLD
CULTURES

EXPLORING WORLD CULTURES

Nepal

Joanne Mattern

Cavendish
Square

New York

Published in 2018 by Cavendish Square Publishing, LLC
243 5th Avenue, Suite 136, New York, NY 10016

Library of Congress Cataloging-in-Publication Data

Names: Mattern, Joanne, 1963- author.
Title: Nepal / Joanne Mattern.
Description: New York : Cavendish Square Publishing, [2018] | Series:
Exploring world cultures | Includes index.
Identifiers: LCCN 2016050904 (print) | LCCN 2016052605 (ebook) |
ISBN 9781502625007 (pbk.) | ISBN 9781502625014 (6 pack) | ISBN 9781502625021
(library bound) | ISBN 9781502625038 (E-book)
Subjects: LCSH: Nepal--Juvenile literature.
Classification: LCC DS493.4 .M37 2017 (print) | LCC DS493.4 (ebook) |
DDC 954.96--dc23
LC record available at https://lccn.loc.gov/2016050904

Editorial Director: David McNamara
Editor: Kristen Susienka
Copy Editor: Rebecca Rohan
Associate Art Director: Amy Greenan
Designer: Joseph Macri
Production Coordinator: Karol Szymczuk
Photo Research: J8 Media

The photographs in this book are used by permission and through the courtesy of: Cover Bartosz Hadyniak/Photodisc/ Getty Images; p. 5, 16 Zzvet/Shutterstock.com; p. 6 Olinchuk/Shutterstock.com; Wang Lama Humla/Wikimedia Commons/ File:Karnali2.jpg/CC BY SA 4.0; p. 8 John Elk III/Lonely Planet Images/Getty Images; p. 9 Binod Joshi/AP Images; p. 10 Xinhua/Alamy Stock Photo; p. 11 Anton Petrus/Moment/Getty Images; p. 12 PRAKASH MATHEMA/AFP/Getty Images; p. 13 Christian Kober/AWL Images/Getty Images; p. 14 Eric Kilby/Wikimedia Commons/File:Snow Leopard Curled (16452939913).jpg.CC BY SA 2.0; p. 15 Feng Wei Photography/Moment Open/Getty Images; p. 18 Kristian Buus/Corbis Historical/Getty Images; p. 19 Btrenkel/iStockphoto.com; p. 20 Alessandro Zappalorto/Shutterstock.com; p. 21 Godong/ Universal Images Group/Getty Images; p. 22 Aexabelov/iStock/Thinkstock.com; p. 24 Archana Shrestha/Pacific Press/ LightRocket/Getty Images; p. 26 SIHASAKPRACHUM/Shutterstock.com; p. 27 Charles Cecil/Alamy Stock Photo; p. 28 Craig Lovell/Eagle Visions Photography/Alamy Stock Photo.

Printed in the United States of America

Contents

Introduction

Nepal is a small country in Asia. It is surrounded by land. Kathmandu is the capital city of Nepal. This city is located near the center of the country.

Nepal is filled with amazing landscapes. Some of the land is flat and wet. The middle of the country has rolling hills. The highest mountains are in northern Nepal. These mountains are called the Himalayas. Mount Everest, the highest mountain in the world, is part of the Himalayas.

More than twenty-nine million people live in Nepal. Nepal's people belong to dozens of **ethnic** groups. Although Nepal's people are very **diverse**, they get along with each other and respect different traditions and cultures.

Nepal has a long and interesting history. Like people all over the world, the Nepalese enjoy sports and games. They spend time with family and friends, and they eat tasty foods. Nepal is an unusual nation with many interesting features.

Two Nepalese girls pose in fancy traditional costumes.

Nepal covers 56,827 square miles (147,181 square kilometers). It is surrounded by India in the west, south, and east. Tibet, which is part of China, lies to the north.

This map shows Nepal's borders and major cities.

The Himalayan Mountains stretch across Nepal's northern border. Many of the world's tallest mountains are in Nepal. The tallest of all is Mount Everest. This mountain rises 29,035 feet (8,850 meters) above sea level.

A Land of Many Rivers

Nepal has many rivers. The most important are the Karnali, Kosi, and Gandaki. These rivers flow down from the Himalayas.

The Karnali River

The southern part of Nepal is a flat area called the Terai. The climate here is hot and wet, and the land is covered with marshes and forests. The middle of Nepal has many rolling hills.

FACT!

A hot wind called the *loo* sometimes blows across the Terai. The loo can raise temperatures as high as 113 degrees Fahrenheit (45 degrees Celsius).

People settled in Nepal as far back as the seventh century BCE. Several different groups ruled Nepal. One of the most important was the Mallas. They ruled from 1200 until the late 1600s.

Durbar Square in Kathmandu

In time, the area around Kathmandu was divided into three kingdoms. A nearby king named Prithvi Narayan Shah spent more than twenty years conquering these kingdoms. By 1768, Shah had combined these kingdoms into the nation of Nepal.

Nepal closed its borders to foreigners between 1816 and 1951.

In 1816, the British conquered Nepal. In 1950, Nepal won its independence and became a **parliamentary democracy**. However, there were many rebellions and changes in the government over the next fifty years.

No More Kings

Nepal was ruled by kings between 1950 and 2007. In 2007, after a lot of fighting, a rebel government got rid of the monarchy, and Nepal became a **republic**.

A picture of the royal family taken in 2001

Nepal was ruled by a monarchy for many years. That changed in 2007 when a new government was formed. This government is ruled by a **legislative** branch with 601 members. Twenty-six members are appointed by

Members get ready for the opening of Parliament in 2015.

the Council of Ministers, 240 are elected by direct popular vote, and 335 are chosen by a percentage of the political party that receives the most votes.

Nepal has five main political parties.

Nepal is divided into fourteen zones, called *anchal*. Each anchal is divided into smaller districts. Each village also has an assembly. Every citizen who is at least eighteen years old can vote in all elections.

There is a lot of fighting between the different parties in Nepal's government. For this reason, the government could not create a **constitution** until 2015.

The Capital City

Kathmandu is the capital of Nepal. More than one million people live there.

The sun rises over the crowded streets of Kathmandu.

Nepal is one of the world's poorest countries. It has few **natural resources** and limited land that can be used for growing crops. Nepal's main crops are rice, corn, wheat, and potatoes. Most farmers cannot produce enough food to feed Nepal's people. Instead, the government must get food from other countries.

A young girl separates grains of wheat by a process called winnowing.

There are few industries in Nepal. The most common are carpet-making, weaving, and handmade wood and leather crafts.

Climbers make their way to a base camp on Mount Everest.

Many tourists come to Nepal to see its natural beauty. Mountain climbing, hiking, and bird watching are popular tourist attractions. Many people in Nepal work as guides or in restaurants and stores that serve tourists.

Pretty Money

Nepal's money is called the rupee. Rupees are colorful paper money that show images of famous people and nature scenes.

Nepal is full of natural beauty. The country has lots of thick forests of bamboo, pine, and oak trees. Many different flowers grow in the hot, wet climate.

The snow leopard is one of Nepal's most beautiful and most endangered animals.

Different animals live in Nepal. Tigers, leopards, elephants, rhinoceroses, and deer live in the Terai. Crocodiles and dolphins swim in the rivers, while storks and cranes live in the marshes. The hills and mountains are also full of life. Himalayan black bears live in the mountains, and so do mountain goats and red pandas.

The rhododendron is Nepal's national flower.

One of Nepal's most beautiful birds is the Indian roller. Many people think it is good luck to spot this bird and its brightly colored wings.

Losing Forests

Nepal's forests are in danger. Between 1950 and 1980, more than half its forests were cut down to provide wood for fuel. Today, Nepal is working hard to save its forests and the animals that live there.

Forests provide life for many animals.

15

About twenty-nine million people live in Nepal. Most of them have an Indian background. Tibetans are another important ethnic group. Hill people, who live in the lower mountains in central and western Nepal, include ethnic groups called the Gurung, Tamang, Rai, and Limbu.

This Tibetan monk is all smiles during the Full Moon Festival.

Nepal's people are divided into groups called castes. The higher the caste, the more comfortable life a person tends to have. Indian Hindus called Brahmins belong to the highest caste. Brahmins are priests and teachers. Lower castes include soldiers, merchants, and people who work in less respected jobs.

FACT!

Although the caste system is slowly disappearing, most people in Nepal still marry, choose jobs, and have friends based on their caste.

The Sherpas

The most famous group of hill people are Sherpas. Sherpas live in the high mountains of the Himalayas. They often serve as guides and helpers for people trying to climb Mount Everest, Earth's highest mountain.

Most of Nepal's people live in the country. Many live in mud or stone homes in the Terai or the hills. They grow their own food and trade with other people for goods and supplies.

This family is from the Chepang tribe.

Kathmandu is Nepal's only major city, although there are several large towns. People in the city live in small houses or apartments. They buy food and other goods in stores. The city streets are filled with buses, taxis, and bicycles.

FACT!

Most children in Nepal start school at age five. School is free, but families have to pay for books and other supplies.

Family is the most important part of society. Most people in Nepal live in extended families. An extended family includes parents, children, grandparents, aunts, uncles, and cousins.

Marriage

Most marriages in Nepal are arranged. Family members bring the bride and groom together. Some couples do not meet until the wedding!

A Nepalese bride on her wedding day

Religion

There are three major religions in Nepal. About 81 percent of the people are Hindu. Eleven percent are Buddhist, and just under 5 percent are Muslim. Many people follow both the Hindu and Buddhist religions.

There are many Buddhist temples in Nepal.

The Hindu religion began in India. Its rules are part of everyday life. Hindus worship hundreds of different gods.

Buddhism is based on the teachings of Siddhartha Gautama, who was called Buddha. He left a life of comfort to find the answers to life.

Buddhists believe that life is an endless cycle of birth, death, and rebirth.

FACT!

Even though they follow different religions and traditions, most people in Nepal respect each other's beliefs.

A Good Life

Hindus believe in reincarnation, or living many lives. They believe that what they do in this life will affect their next life. If a person does good deeds, he or she will have a better position in the next life.

Hindus worship many gods.

Nepali is the national language of Nepal. Nepali is a lot like the Hindi language that is spoken in India. Nepali first appeared in the twelfth century. This language is taught in schools, along with English.

Nepalese writing is very fancy and beautiful!

Because it is so difficult to travel from one part of Nepal to another, people in different parts of the country speak different dialects.

Most people in Nepal also speak a local language, or dialect. The hill people speak a language that is a lot like Chinese. This language also uses a different form of writing than Nepali does.

Choose Your Words Carefully!

When speaking Nepali, people use different words depending on who they are talking to. Some words show respect and are used when a person is speaking to someone who is more important than he or she is. There are even special words used to speak to the royal family.

Nepal is filled with artistic treasures! There are many beautiful statues all over Nepal, especially in Kathmandu. Most of Nepal's art is based on religion. Paintings and statues show religious themes and important figures.

A group of men play traditional Nepalese instruments.

Music is very popular in Nepal. People play flutes, drums, and a traditional horn called a *shehnai*. Western music and instruments, such as guitars and banjos, are also popular. Music is a big part of any festival, wedding, or other celebration.

Dashain is the biggest holiday in Nepal. It celebrates good winning over evil. Dashain celebrations last for fifteen days.

Nepal's New Year celebrations begin in the middle of April. People fill the streets and play traditional music.

The Festival of Lights

Tihar is a fall festival that comes right after Dashain. During Tihar, people light their homes to honor Laxmi, the goddess of wealth and good fortune.

25

Fun and Play

People in Nepal work very hard, but they also like to have fun! Sports are very popular in Nepal. Kite flying is enjoyed by children and adults. People have kite battles, where they try to snap

Boys fly kites on a hill in Nepal.

the string of another kite with the sharp string of their own kite. People in Nepal also enjoy *kabaddi*, which is a type of tag played by two teams.

Most people in Nepal do not have televisions or radios.

People who live in Nepal's towns love to go to the movies. Most movies come from India. They are full of action, comedy, music, and beautiful costumes.

Tigers and Goats

Nepal's most famous board game is called *bagh-chal*, or "tigers and goats." The player who is the tiger uses his or her pieces to jump over the other player's goats, while the goats try to trap the tigers so they cannot move.

The game board for Tigers and Goats

Food

Rice is the most important and popular food in Nepal. It is eaten at every meal. The most common meal is a spicy lentil soup with rice and vegetables, called *daal bhaat*. Potatoes and squash are also common foods. Many people enjoy potatoes dipped in salt and hot chilies.

A young Nepalese girl enjoys a meal of rice.

FACT!

Hindus are not allowed to eat beef.

Many foods in Nepal originally came from other countries. Dumplings filled with meat come from Tibet and China. Many people also enjoy Indian flatbreads.

Meat is a rare treat in most of Nepal. The most common meats come from buffalo, goats, or yaks.

Tea is the most popular drink in Nepal. It can be hot and spicy or sweet. People also enjoy milk and yogurt drinks.

The Right Way to Eat

Food is only eaten with the right hand. People scoop up food with this hand and pop it in their mouths.

Glossary

constitution A document that describes a country's laws.

diverse Different.

ethnic People who have a common culture or ancestry.

legislative The part of the government that passes laws.

natural resources Materials found in the earth, like gas and coal, that are used to make cars move or to heat homes.

parliamentary democracy A form of government in which the party that controls the legislature leads the government.

republic A state where power is held by the people and their elected representatives.

Find Out More

Books

Burbank, John. *Cultures of the World: Nepal*.

New York: Cavendish Square Publishing, 2014.

Owings, Lisa. *Nepal*. Mankato, MN: Bellwether

Media, 2014.

Website

National Geographic Kids: Nepal

http://kids.nationalgeographic.com/explore/

countries/nepal/#nepal-himalayas.jpg

Video

A Peek Into the Life of Nepali Schoolchildren

https://youtu.be/DxSE_aEpJh8

This video was created by students to show what

their lives in Nepal are like.

Index

About the Author

Joanne Mattern is the author of more than 250 books for children. She specializes in writing nonfiction and has explored many different places in her writing. Her favorite topics include history, travel, sports, biography, and animals. Mattern lives in New York State with her husband, four children, and several pets.